DON'T KNOW MUCH ABOUT®

MUMMIES

KENNETH C. DAVIS
ILLUSTRATED BY S. D. SCHINDLER

HarperCollins Publishers

ALSO BY KENNETH C. DAVIS

PICTURE BOOKS:
Don't Know Much About® the 50 States
Don't Know Much About® the Solar System
Don't Know Much About® the Presidents
Don't Know Much About® the Kings and Queens of England
Don't Know Much About® the Pilgrims
Don't Know Much About® the Pioneers
Don't Know Much About® Dinosaurs

MIDDLE-GRADE TITLES:
Don't Know Much About® Planet Earth
Don't Know Much About® Space
Don't Know Much About® American History
Don't Know Much About® World Myths

BIOGRAPHIES:
Don't Know Much About® George Washington
Don't Know Much About® Sitting Bull
Don't Know Much About® Abraham Lincoln
Don't Know Much About® Rosa Parks
Don't Know Much About® Thomas Jefferson

An author's name goes on the cover of a book. But behind that book are a great many people who make it all happen. I especially thank April Prince for her devoted efforts and unique contributions. This book would not have been possible without her tireless work, imagination, and creativity.

This is a Don't Know Much About® book. Don't Know Much About® is the trademark of Kenneth C. Davis.

Don't Know Much About® Mummies
Copyright © 2005 by Kenneth C. Davis

Manufactured in China by South China Printing Company Ltd.
All rights reserved.
www.harperchildrens.com

Library of Congress Cataloging-in-Publication Data
Davis, Kenneth C.
  Don't know much about mummies / Kenneth C. Davis ; illustrated by S. D. Schindler.—1st ed.
    p.   cm. — (Don't know much about)
  ISBN 0-06-028781-0 — ISBN 0-06-028782-9 (lib. bdg.)
  1. Mummies. I. Schindler, S. D., ill. II. Title. III. Series.
GN293.D38 2005   2004004124
393'.3—dc22

Design by Charles Yuen

1 2 3 4 5 6 7 8 9 10
❖
First Edition

Say the word *mummy* to most people and they think about scary monster movies with a creepy dead guy wrapped up in a bunch of nasty old bandages. And they will almost always think about ancient Egypt, home to some of the world's most famous mummies. Unless they are from England, where *mummy* is another word for "mom."

But mummies are much more than creatures from a monster movie or even ancient Egyptians. And sometimes they might actually be somebody's mother.

Instead of just scaring us, mummies can be really great teachers. Not the kind of teacher who stands in front of your classroom and teaches you math and reading, though. Mummies can be very good at telling us all about what life was like a long time ago—even though they can't talk. They can show us how tall people were, what people used to eat, how they may have dressed, the kinds of jobs they did, and what kind of religion they may have practiced. That's a lot to learn from somebody who can't speak and possibly couldn't read or write.

Most of us have an idea about what a mummy is—usually based on what we have seen on television or maybe at a museum. But the whole truth about mummies is a lot more interesting than what you may think. Basically, a mummy is a dead person—or animal—whose body has been preserved, either by nature or by some artificial method. While some of the most famous mummies do come wrapped up in layers of cloth bandages, scientists have also discovered mummies who were frozen in ice, trapped in dry caves without air, or even buried in mud. As scientists have studied these preserved bodies over the years, with microscopes and X-ray machines and other tools, they have learned an enormous amount about what life was like long ago, sometimes before there were any written records.

Don't Know Much About® *Mummies* tells the inside story about who these fascinating real people were and how they became mummies. I think you'll agree that the truth about mummies is a lot more interesting than the made-up stories you see at the movies.

WHAT ARE MUMMIES?

A mummy is a dead body that is:

a) scary
b) wrapped in linen bandages
c) made in Egypt
d) more than just a skeleton

The answer is *d.* The best-known mummies are those of ancient Egyptian kings and queens. Wrapped in bandages, they were buried in fancy tombs or giant pyramids. But mummies don't have to be Egyptian, and they don't have to be wrapped in cloth. They don't even have to be kings or queens. A mummy is simply any dead body whose soft parts did not *decay*, or rot away. A mummy might have most or part of its skin, hair, heart, brain, lungs, and more.

Do most dead bodies become mummies?

No. In fact, very few do. It takes special conditions to make a mummy.

Normally, when a person or animal dies, its body quickly begins to rot. Dead things decay because tiny living creatures called *bacteria* grow in dead bodies and eat their tissues. Soon all that's left is a skeleton. Bacteria need air and water to live, and they especially love warm, moist places. They don't grow well in very dry or freezing cold areas. That's why mummies are usually frozen or dried. (That's also why food keeps longer in the refrigerator or freezer than it does on the kitchen countertop.)

Nice and moist!

This is perfect!

...and plenty of air!

Not too cold!

Good times!

Who made the finest mummies of all?

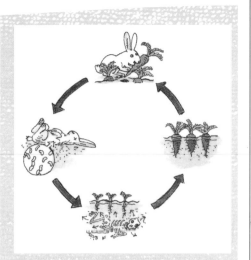

Nature. Some of the best preserved and oldest mummies we have found were made by the natural processes of earth and air. (That's actually how the first Egyptian mummies were made.) These mummies were bodies that had been left in dry or freezing-cold air, hot sand, ice, or in a place with no air at all. These conditions kept bacteria from doing their job and created mummies that were just as good, or sometimes even better, than those made by humans.

Decay is the way nature recycles living matter into the earth. Decayed bodies feed the earth by making fertile soil where new plants can grow. Those plants become food for animals. If dead things didn't rot, imagine how cluttered the world would be!

 TRUE OR FALSE Mummies have been found all over the world.

True. The ancient Egyptians made some of the most famous mummies known. But the Egyptians weren't alone. (And they weren't the first—you'll find out who was on page 30.) People have found mummies around the world, from Australia to China to Peru. Many cultures created mummies because they believed there was another life after death. Preserving a person's body was a way to ensure that his or her spirit lived on in the next life. Other civilizations believed mummies were an important link between the living and the dead.

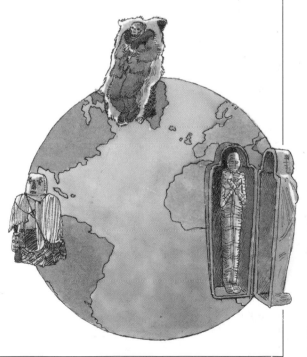

LIFE AND DEATH IN EGYPT

Why did the Egyptians make mummies?

Ancient Egypt was one of the first, and greatest, civilizations in the world. Egyptians loved their way of life so much that they wanted it to go on as long as possible. To them, death was just the gateway to the next world. There, all the good parts of Egyptian life became better and all the bad parts disappeared.

Life in Egypt *was* pretty great. The weather was almost always sunny and warm. The Nile River, which created fertile farmland when it flooded its banks every year, provided everyone with plenty of fish, vegetables, fruits, and grain for bread and beer. The fertile land also gave Egyptians the papyrus plant for making a kind of paper, the flax plant for weaving fine linen cloth, and mud for making bricks and pottery. Beyond the farmland was the desert that held gold, semiprecious gems, and stone for building.

Since the Egyptians had plenty of food at hand, they had time to devote to things other than farming. They invented both a calendar and one of the first forms of writing. They built some of the most amazing stone structures in the world, including the pyramids. They studied medicine, astronomy, and engineering, and had a highly developed religion.

How old are Egypt's mummies?

Egyptians were making mummies almost five thousand years ago! The amazing Egyptian civilization lasted about three thousand years, a span so long that historians usually divide it into a number of periods. The earliest begins about five thousand years ago, around 3000 B.C.E., with the first pharaohs. The last period ends in about 30 B.C.E., when Queen Cleopatra died and the Roman Empire took over the country.

B.C.E. means "Before the Common Era." It's a way of labeling dates in early history. If you like to count backward, you'll like B.C.E. It starts before the Common Era, or C.E. (in which we live), and goes back in time. So 100 B.C.E. means one hundred years before the Common Era, and 2000 B.C.E. is two thousand years before the Common Era. When you reach 1 B.C.E., the next year is 1 C.E., and you start counting forward to the present day.

Why are Egyptian mummies so famous?

Egyptians made millions of mummies, and a number of them are beautiful and intricate works of art. The Egyptians took mummy-making seriously. They believed that a person needed a body so that his or her soul could live on in the Land of the Dead.

The Egyptians believed that everyone had three souls: the *ba*, the *ka*, and the *akh*. When a person died, his or her *ba* and *ka* were freed from the body and lived on in the burial tomb. The *ba* traveled back and forth from the body to the other world, keeping contact with living friends and relatives. The *ka* stayed in the body as the person's life force. Eventually the *ba* and *ka* would join together to form an *akh,* an immortal godlike spirit. If the *ba* could not recognize the body and be reunited with the *ka* in the tomb, the person would not live forever. So Egyptians tried hard to keep their dead bodies not only preserved, but also looking lifelike.

How did the Egyptians know how to make mummies?

They learned from nature. Early Egyptians were buried in simple sand pits, where the hot desert sand dried out their bodies and created natural mummies. When Egyptians realized this, they decided to improve on nature. First they tried putting their dead in wood coffins to better preserve their bodies. But this had the opposite effect. Since the hot, dry sand could not soak up the moisture from bodies in coffins, the bodies decayed. The Egyptians tried and tried until they got the process right. Over hundreds of years, they perfected the art of mummification.

Were all Egyptians mummified?

Most were, but the method depended on the family's wealth and status. The poor had simple pit burials because mummification was a long and expensive process. Pharaohs—kings of Egypt—and other nobles who could afford it were painstakingly mummified and buried. The richer the pharaoh, the more decorated his mummy.

MAKING MUMMIES

How long did it take to make an Egyptian mummy?

Seventy days. The priests who were the *embalmers*, or people who preserve dead bodies, spent the first sixteen days cleaning out the body. First, they cleansed and purified it. Then they made a slit in the belly and removed the dead person's lungs, intestines, liver, and stomach. They did this because the internal organs were the first things to rot. (The heart, however, always remained inside the dead person. Egyptians believed the heart was the center of thought and feeling and would be needed in the next life.) Then the embalmers rinsed out the chest and abdomen with palm wine. They dried each removed organ, wrapped it in linen, and either placed it in a separate *canopic jar*, or minicoffin, or put it back into the body once it dried out.

Each canopic jar was topped with the figure of a particular god, who was supposed to protect the organ inside. There was *Hapi*, for the lungs; *Duamutef*, for the stomach; *Imsety*, for the liver; and *Qebhsenuf*, for the intestines.

What became of a mummy's brain?

It was thrown away because it was thought to have no value. But getting the brain out of the head was no easy feat. Since Egyptians wanted the mummy to look lifelike, they couldn't harm the face or skull. So embalmers took the brain out through the nose! Using hooks inserted through the nostrils, they broke up the brain, scooped out the pieces, and let the rest drain out through the nose.

Did Egyptians prefer their mummies salted?

Yes, but not for eating. (Yuck!) They used salt to dry out the mummies. After the first sixteen days, once the body was clean, embalmers placed it on a slanted embalming board and covered it with *natron*, a natural salt that soaks up water and helps kill bacteria. Fluids dripped out of the body and into a container at the foot of the board. Many embalmers also placed packs of natron inside the body.

What do mummies have in common with raisins?

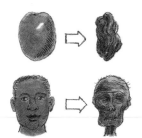

They're both dry and shriveled! As the natron soaked up water, it also shrank the body. After forty days, the priests cleaned and massaged the dried body with sweet-smelling spices and perfumes. To make the skin soft again, they rubbed in oils or sometimes even wine or milk. Then they coated the skin with a sticky substance called *resin* that kept bacteria from growing.

The treated mummy was stuffed with linen pads and sawdust. (This kept the body from collapsing like a glove with no hand inside.) Then the embalmers sealed the slit in the belly. They plugged the nostrils with beeswax and filled the eye sockets with onions or pieces of pottery so they would keep their shape.

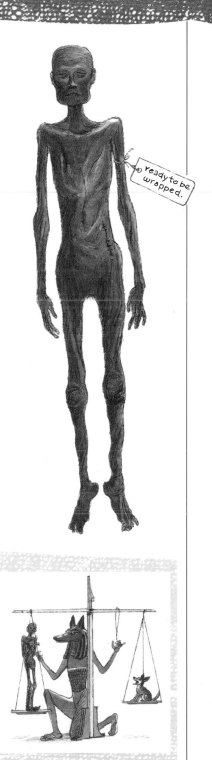

ready to be wrapped.

How did mummies get their name?

Oh, my! You must have fallen into a big hole full of moumia!

Not from their children, but from Arabs, who conquered Egypt in 604. The Arabs found mummies that had been made after the kingdom of Egypt began to decline in wealth about three thousand years ago. By this time embalmers made mummies less carefully. They pumped the bodies full of resin, which darkened over time and made mummies look like they were covered with tar. When Arabs discovered some of these mummies, they thought they were covered with *bitumen,* a tarlike substance that turns shiny and hard when it dries. The Arabic word for bitumen was *moumia,* so people began calling these bodies mummies.

After the natron did its job, the dried, shrunken body weighed only about as much as a small dog.

WRAPPING A MUMMY

What did a well-dressed mummy wear?

As many as twenty layers of cloth. Priests bound mummies with long strips of linen. They wrapped the head, torso, hands, and feet, covering each finger and toe separately. Sometimes the fingers and toes were capped with gold. Then the priests wrapped the legs together, put pads on top of the torso to round it out, and wrapped the entire mummy again. Finally they added *shrouds*, large pieces of material that covered the mummy from head to toe, and held them in place with more bandages brushed with resin.

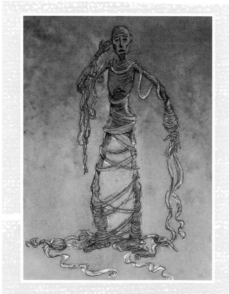

Why don't mummies like to relax?

They're afraid they'll unwind.

What do mummies like to listen to?

Wrap music!

12

Did priests whistle while they worked?

No, but they did chant spells. As they chanted, the priests tucked *amulets*, or magic charms, between the mummy's wrappings. (Later mummies had spells written on their outer shroud as well.) Amulets were supposed to protect the mummy and ward off evil spirits, and they were worn by the living as well as the dead. Each had a different meaning. The scarab beetle meant rebirth; *udjat,* or the protective Eye of Horus, was the symbol of healing; and a *djed*-pillar was endurance and stability. The amulets were made from various semiprecious stones, each of which gave the charms different powers.

That's our finest, sire! On sale for 2 gold pieces/yd.

Ooh! Nice feel! I'd die for this!

Since all cloth was woven by hand in ancient Egypt, only the mummies of the richest people were wrapped in specially woven linen. Poorer people were wrapped in old clothes or even ships' sails that had been shredded into strips.

Did mummy-makers ever make mistakes?

Yes. Sometimes embalmers stuffed bodies too tightly and caused them to burst. Other times, a mummy's ear, arm, or leg fell off. If the body part wasn't collected and put into a special jar to be buried with the mummy, it was tucked inside the mummy's bandages. But since many embalming workshops were busy places, sometimes a missing part was tucked in with the wrong mummy, without anyone knowing it!

CASES AND COFFINS

Why were mummies always ready for Halloween?

Because they wore masks. But unlike Halloween masks, mummies' masks were meant to make their owners look more like they had in life. This was so their *ba* would recognize them. The masks of most mummies were golden or painted, but after Egypt became part of the Roman Empire in 30 B.C.E., flat paintings replaced the masks. Just in case the mask didn't do its job, the name of the mummified person was also written on the mummy's linen strips and on its coffin cases.

Could mummies see out of their coffins?

No. But Egyptians thought they could. Early Egyptians buried their mummies in rectangular wooden coffins that had eyes painted on the side. Sometimes the mummy was placed on its side in the coffin, facing east, so it could "see" the rising sun through the painted eyes. The coffin also had the person's name on the lid and *hieroglyphics*, the picture-writing of the ancient Egyptians, around the sides, end, and lid.

Later mummies were buried in *mummiform*, or mummy-shaped, coffins—sometimes two or three coffins one inside another! Each coffin was supposed to give the mummy more spiritual and physical protection. Each was painted inside and out with pictures of gods and goddesses and magic spells written in *hieroglyphs*, the picture-symbols that made up hieroglyphic writing.

I'm back. How have you been, Ka?

Why did mummies' coffins have a coffin of their own?

For even more protection. The nested coffins were sometimes placed in a huge stone coffin called a *sarcophagus*. A sarcophagus was very expensive and very, very heavy. Only pharaohs or other high-ranking people were buried inside them.

How do we know what ancient Egyptian hieroglyphs say?

For more than a thousand years, we didn't know. But the mystery was unraveled in 1822. Hieroglyphics, the earliest form of Egyptian writing, died out when another kind of writing, called *demotic*, was invented around 600 B.C.E. In 1799 a French soldier found a black stone slab, later called the Rosetta Stone, in Egypt. The Rosetta Stone was inscribed with three kinds of writing: hieroglyphics, demotic, and Greek. Scholars soon realized that the three sections of writing represented the same text in three different languages, although Greek was the only one still understood. A Frenchman named Jean-François Champollion spent most of his life trying to decode the Rosetta Stone by comparing the Greek to the other texts. His success in 1822 allowed *Egyptologists*, or scientists who study ancient Egypt, to understand the writings on statues, tombs, temples, and mummy cases.

Even in ancient Egypt, only about one in twenty people understood hieroglyphics. And no wonder—the writing had more than seven hundred different symbols! Hieroglyphics were mostly used as inscriptions on monuments, temple walls, and tombs.

You can try your own hand at reading hieroglyphs. Because some symbols stood for one letter, others for a combination of letters, and still others for entire words, there was more than one correct way to write a word or phrase. One way to write the name Ramses II is shown at the right. The first character is the sound "ra," the second is "mes," and the third, repeated, character is "s." The *cartouche*, or oval loop, around the hieroglyphs shows that the name belongs to a royal person.

◎ = ra

⍟ = m

∩∩ = ss

Did an Egyptian mummy travel to its funeral in style?

It depended (like everything else) on the dead person's status and wealth. You could tell a person's importance by how big and fancy his or her funeral procession was.

FUNERAL PROCESSION

Funerals were important events in ancient Egypt. A funeral procession was like a parade. Family, friends, priests, and servants carried the items that would be buried with the mummy. (Tombs were stocked with all kinds of wonderful things. You'll read about that on pages 21, 25, and 26.) The procession included professional mourners, who were paid to wail and cry and throw dust on themselves to show grief. Oxen pulled the mummy itself across the sand in an elaborate sled. The canopic jars, inside a wooden canopic chest, rode on their own sled.

The funeral procession traveled from the dead person's house to his or her burial site. Egyptians built their tombs in the desert, where the land could not be used for farming.

Was there a dentist at the funeral?

No, but at the tomb a priest did hold a ceremony called the "Opening of the Mouth." The mummy's mouth wasn't actually opened, but the priest magically gave it the ability to speak, eat, and taste again. In the same way the priest opened the eyes to see, the nose to breathe, and the ears to hear. After the ceremony the mummy was put in its sarcophagus, which was

covered with a heavy stone lid. The mourners left, and the entrance to the tomb was tightly sealed. Later, priestesses and family members would bring food offerings for the mummy's *ka,* as a way of honoring the life force and keeping it alive.

What did the dead person have to do to reach the afterlife?

After the funeral, according to the Egyptians, the dead person's soul began the dangerous journey to the Land of the Dead. To be accepted there, a dead person had his or her heart weighed against the "feather of truth." If the heart was heavy with sins and outweighed the feather, the monstrous Ammut, Devourer of the Dead, ate the heart.

PYRAMIDS AND TOMBS

Were all pharaohs buried in pyramids?

No. In fact, only a few were. The earliest tombs weren't pyramids, but rather rectangular brick structures called *mastabas*. Builders placed mastabas over burial chambers dug deep into the ground.

As Egypt grew richer and more powerful, a pharaoh named Djoser wanted something more outstanding. Around 2600 B.C.E., Djoser's architect thought of stacking up six stone mastabas, each smaller than the one under it. The architect had invented the step pyramid. His building looked like a stairway to the stars and therefore to the afterlife. Later, Egyptians began to build true pyramids, with smooth sides created by filling in the areas between the steps. The smooth sides, believed to represent the rays of the sun, were thought to be a link to the heavens. Remains of about one hundred royal pyramids have been found in Egypt.

 TRUE OR FALSE Construction of a ruler's tomb often began while he or she was alive.

True. Since most Egyptians didn't live past the age of forty, it made more sense to prepare for the life after death, which would last forever, than for old age on earth. Plus, some pyramids were so big and complicated that they took twenty years to build! A ruler couldn't afford to wait until he died to get things started.

The Great Pyramid is the largest of the three most famous pyramids in the world—the pyramids at Giza. When it was built more than four thousand years ago, the Great Pyramid was 481 feet high. (That's three times as high as the Statue of Liberty in New York!) The base would have covered six football fields.

The Great Pyramid originally held more than 2.3 million blocks of stone, each weighing, on average, five thousand pounds. Today the limestone that once covered the outside of the pyramids has been removed, and some of the underlying stone has worn away. But the pyramids are still a massive, amazing sight.

The Great Pyramid at Giza in Egypt is the only one of the Seven Wonders of the Ancient World still standing. Near it is the famous Great Sphinx. (A *sphinx* is an imaginary creature with the body of a lion and the head of a person, hawk, or ram.) Sphinxes were supposed to be powerful defenders of the king, and of good over evil.

How did the Egyptians build the pyramids?

No one knows for sure. But we do know that they must have used a lot of muscle power, because the Egyptians had no complex machines, pulleys, or even wheels to make their job easier.

We know that there were thousands upon thousands of workers. These laborers weren't slaves, as many people think, but mostly farmers who built pyramids during the flood season, when they couldn't work on their farms. They worked as a way of paying their taxes to the pharaoh. They also believed that building the pyramids would help them get to the next life.

The workers cut huge chunks of rock out of the desert. Then they pulled the massive stones up ramps, which were built higher and higher as the pyramid grew taller.

Before workers began building a pyramid, they had to *level*, or flatten out, the site. Then they aligned its sides perfectly to the north, south, east, and west. This was done so that the pharaoh's spirit would be able to get its bearings for the journey to the afterlife.

Now I've got my bearings!

STOCKING THE TOMB

 Egyptian tombs were often like palaces.

True. A tomb was meant to be a person's home in death—a home forever. So tombs often had many rooms and were richly decorated.

Since Egyptians believed the next life would be much like the one they knew, they filled tombs with everything the person might need. That could include furniture, food, clothing, musical instruments, board games, makeup, wigs, and mirrors, among other objects. They also buried fine things with the dead person to show the person's social class. These helped ensure that the dead person would be treated with respect in the afterlife.

Statues of the dead person were put in the tomb. That way, if anything happened to the person's mummy, his or her *ba* and *ka* would still have a place to rest.

You're not my mummy, but hey, you'll do!

Did tombs have wallpaper?

No. They had something even better. Artists painted the walls of tombs with beautiful murals that showed scenes from the dead person's daily life. Egyptians thought the scenes would magically come to life. They showed the person hunting, playing games, eating and drinking, and enjoying time with family and friends. These tomb paintings are part of the reason we know so much about ancient Egyptian life today.

Were Egyptian servants buried with their masters?

No, but Egyptians did create *ushabti* figures, or small pottery models of people, to represent the dead person's servants. These servants would do the hard work in the afterlife so the dead person wouldn't have to. Spells written on the *ushabtis* would make them answer when the dead person was called upon to work in the fields. (*Ushabti* means "answerer.") Some tombs held hundreds of *ushabtis,* one for every day of the year.

TOMB RAIDERS

Why wouldn't a pharaoh want to be buried in a pyramid?

As magnificent as pyramids were, they were also enormous advertisements for the riches that were inside. Tomb raiders found ways to get in, even though tunnels, false entrances, dead ends, and traps had been built to confuse them. About 3,500 years ago, pharaohs began to have their tombs built in a faraway, empty valley that was named the Valley of the Kings. In the valley, builders cut tunnels and even the tombs themselves into the rock, hidden from sight. The entrances there were tightly sealed and heavily guarded. Sadly, even those tombs were not safe.

Who were the first tomb raiders?

Often, they were family members of the original tomb builders. These people knew where and how the tombs had been built. And these raiders not only took the mummy's treasures, but they also often unwrapped the mummy itself to look for precious amulets or other riches. They had no respect for the mummy or its resting place. Of the millions of Egyptian mummies made, very few survive today.

TRUE OR FALSE

Mummies make great medicine.

False. But that's not what people would have said in the Middle Ages. By the 1500s, few mummies were left because many had been taken from tombs and ground up to make a medicine called mummy powder. This powder was thought to cure upset stomachs, coughs, bruises, broken bones, and other ailments. It was also supposed to give longer life. In reality swallowing mummy powder often made people throw up and gave them awful stomach cramps—not to mention bad breath!

Do mummies make good souvenirs?

Some Europeans thought so. European travelers who went to Egypt in the 1800s and early 1900s sometimes brought mummies home with them. Then they sold tickets to mummy unwrappings. They didn't expect the mummy to get up and dance, of course, but they thought it was fun to see what was underneath all that linen. Would they find jewels and a lifelike body, or beetles and a skeleton? Most of these Europeans weren't trying to study or learn from mummies. They just wanted to put on a show. They didn't respect mummies any more than tomb raiders had. When the show was over, they usually just threw away the mummy and its wrappings.

At some mummy unwrappings, people must have held their noses. Mummies can smell really awful if they haven't been well preserved and have rotted over time. But most don't smell bad. Instead they have a sweet smell from all the herbs and resin used to make them.

RAMSES II

What great mummy discovery was made in 1881?

In that year a museum assistant named Émile Brugsch followed an Egyptian guide into an unmarked chamber above the Valley of the Kings. There, in a room cut deep into the cliffs, he found forty royal mummies. Among them was Ramses II, known today as Ramses the Great. Though the tomb and mummies had been raided of their riches long before, the mummies were still there. Ramses had been secretly reburied in the chamber a few hundred years after his death, after his own tomb in the Valley of the Kings was robbed.

Was Ramses really Great?

Ramses ruled for sixty-six years, a very long time in ancient Egypt, where few people even lived that long. (Ramses lived to be almost ninety!) During his reign, which began in 1279 B.C.E., Egypt was a strong and wealthy empire. Ramses built one of the largest armies the world had ever seen. He used it to conquer countries that had valuable things like slaves, ivory, weapons, rare woods, leopard skins, and gold. Ramses also built more monuments to himself and fathered more children—more than one hundred, with his many wives—than any other Egyptian pharaoh in history.

Why did Ramses fly to Paris three thousand years after his death?

Like anyone who travels out of his or her country, Ramses needed a passport. His passport gave his occupation as "King (deceased)." As a king, Ramses was greeted by an honor guard and a full military salute when he arrived at the airport in Paris in 1976!

Ramses needed to go to the doctor. Several years after Ramses was found, his discoverers unwrapped and examined him. Then they put him on display at a museum in Cairo, Egypt. Over the years, fungi that were accidentally brought into the museum by visitors began to grow on his unwrapped body. In 1976 the body was flown from Cairo to experts in Paris who repaired and sterilized it so that it would not decay any more.

KING TUT

Have scientists ever found a pharaoh's tomb that hadn't been raided?

By the time scientists found the mummy of Ramses the Great, explorers had already discovered most of the pharaohs' tombs. Every tomb had already been robbed. But an English *archaeologist* named Howard Carter wondered about the tomb of the boy king Tutankhamen. (An archaeologist is a person who studies ancient times and peoples by looking at what those people left behind.) Tutankhamen had become pharaoh at the age of nine and died when he was about eighteen. So far, his tomb had not turned up.

Carter was determined to find King Tut's tomb. In 1922 Carter's workers looked through the one small part of the Valley of the Kings that had not been thoroughly searched. Sure enough, the workers found a staircase buried beneath the sand. Sixteen narrow steps led down to a doorway. Behind the doorway was a passage and a stone door bearing King Tut's seal. Those doors had been broken through and resealed three thousand years before, but most of Tut's tomb was still intact.

What was in Tut's tomb?

Inside Tut's tomb, Carter found the ground scattered with beads, as well as a scarf holding gold rings. It looked as if the ancient tomb raiders had left in a hurry. But many other treasures had not been touched. The tomb contained clothing and shoes, furniture that included a throne inlaid with gold, musical instruments, tools, weapons, food and wine,

When Howard Carter chipped a hole through the door that showed King Tut's seal and stuck his candle in, his financial sponsor, an Englishman named Lord Carnarvon, asked, "Can you see anything?" Carter replied, "Yes. Wonderful things!" Later Carter said that when his eyes adjusted to the dim light, he had seen "strange animals, statues, and gold—everywhere the glint of gold."

King Tut's tomb was the greatest archaeological find of the past hundred years. The discovery made people, especially in England, Tutankhamen-crazy. The tomb's treasures inspired new fashions in clothing, jewelry, furniture, and art. Today the artifacts are in the Cairo Museum, and King Tut's mummy rests back in its tomb.

bouquets of flowers, chariots, a fleet of model boats, and statues of King Tut and of gods and goddesses.

The finest treasure of all—King Tut himself—was in a separate room. The pharaoh was buried in a huge golden shrine that contained three inner shrines. Inside those, a stone sarcophagus held three nested coffins. The innermost coffin was made of solid gold. King Tut's mummy wore a solid gold mask that some people say is the most beautiful historical artifact ever found. Tut also wore gold sandals on his feet, and his toes and fingers were covered with gold caps. If this was the tomb of a young, relatively unimportant king, what must have been inside the tombs of Egypt's greatest kings?

Did King Tut start the "Mummy's Curse"?

No, but some people say he did. Howard Carter was so careful about taking notes and preserving everything in the tomb that it took him six years to study it all. With the Tutankhamen craze, some journalists got impatient with Carter. They began to make up stories that said King Tut had put a curse on anyone who entered his tomb. They said that there was a tablet inside the tomb that read, "Death shall come on swift wings to him who toucheth the tomb of Pharaoh." (No such tablet was ever found.) Why else, they said, would robbers leave all the treasure

and re-seal the tomb's doors behind them? (In fact, the tomb was sealed by priests after the thieves had been caught.)

The legend of the Mummy's Curse grew when Lord Carnarvon, the first person to enter the tomb in 1922, died five months later of an infected mosquito bite. A rumor said that at the moment of Carnarvon's death, every light in Cairo went out for five minutes. In fact, the lights in the *hospital* did go out for a few moments, but even today it's not rare for the lights in Cairo to go out without warning. Another rumor said that Carnarvon's dog Susie, back in England, howled once and dropped dead at the moment of Carnarvon's death. (Carter, however, who spent so much time in the tomb, lived a normal, healthy life and died seventeen years after the excavation, at the age of sixty-four.) What do *you* think of the Mummy's Curse?

Who made the most exciting Egyptian mummy discovery since King Tut's tomb?

A donkey! The animal accidentally put its foot through the roof of a tomb in 1996, leading archaeologists to a site they named the Valley of the Golden Mummies. There archaeologists found a huge burial ground that might hold as many as ten thousand ancient mummies. The excavation, the largest ever done in Egypt, is expected to take fifty years. The mummies are from wealthy, though not royal, families, and many are covered with a thin layer of gold. Most of the bodies are about two thousand years old and date from a time when Egypt was controlled by Greece and Rome. The Greeks and Romans adopted the ancient Egyptian tradition of mummy-making but changed it a little to suit their own customs. They often wrapped their mummies in complex patterns and painted lifelike death masks. Many of the mummies hold a coin in their hands to pay the ferryman to the underworld.

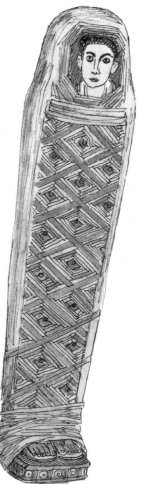

ANIMAL MUMMIES

Did Egyptian mummies keep pets?

Yes, sometimes a favorite pet was mummified and placed in the tomb to keep its owner company in the next life. More often people mummified animals for religious reasons. Many Egyptian gods were linked to animals. For example, a bird called the *ibis* has a beak shaped like a crescent moon, so Egyptians honored the bird as the symbol of the moon god, Thoth. They left the animal mummies in temples as offerings to the gods they represented. In fact, they raised some animals specifically to be made into mummies. Egyptians mummified cats, crocodiles, birds, fish, mice, snakes, dogs, bulls, monkeys, and even an egg with the same care they used with people.

What was the purr-fect Egyptian pet?

A cat. Cats were especially honored in ancient Egypt. Anyone who killed a cat could be punished by death! When a pet cat died, the people in the house shaved their eyebrows in mourning. Cats were sacred to the goddess Bastet, and great numbers of them were mummified and buried in huge cemeteries around temples devoted to the goddess. Scientists think that, over the years, Egyptians must have made millions of cat mummies.

What's the oldest mummy ever found?

It's not an Egyptian, but a natural mummy of an insect preserved in *amber*, or fossilized resin from plants. It's 310 million years old, which means it's older than the first dinosaurs! In the movie *Jurassic Park*, scientists used blood from an insect preserved in this kind of resin to re-create dinosaurs. (The insect was supposed to have bitten a dinosaur, and therefore had dinosaur blood inside it.) In truth, dinosaur blood couldn't have been preserved well enough for this to happen.

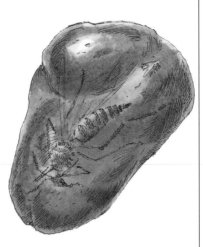

Who is Blue Babe?

Blue Babe is the natural mummy of a 36,000-year-old bison that was found in Alaska in 1979. Babe got his name because a mineral in the soil had turned his skin blue.

Other very old (but not as colorful) animal mummies include those of woolly mammoths. Woolly mammoths were a type of elephant that used to live in northern Europe, northern Asia, and North America. Mammoths are now *extinct*, or no longer living, so their mummies, preserved in frozen ground, give scientists a rare glimpse of these long-ago creatures. One baby mammoth found in Siberia, Russia, in 1977 is thought to be 40,000 years old.

You be careful! Do you want to end up a mummy?

Some mummies were made like stick figures.

True. About seven thousand years ago, at least two thousand years before the Egyptians began making mummies, a group we call the Chinchorro people of Chile created the first artificial mummies we know about. The Chinchorro basically took the dead person's body apart, dried it out, and put it back together on a stick frame.

SOUTH AMERICA— CHINCHORRO AND PARACAS MUMMIES

First, the Chinchorro removed the dead person's head, arms, and legs. Then they peeled the skin back, probably placing it in seawater to keep it soft. After taking out the internal organs and brain, they dried the inside of the body with hot coals and removed and cleaned the arm and leg bones.

Then the Chinchorro put the body on a stick frame, tying all the pieces together with reed cords. They stuffed the chest with grass and ash and padded the body with grass, feathers, and other material. A thick paste made from ash was spread all over the body, and the skin was pulled back on. (If it didn't fit, the Chinchorro patched it with animal skin.) They glued a wig to the head and painted a clay mask with mineral paint. The whole body was then painted black or red and buffed to a shine.

The body of a Chinchorro boy who died in about 5000 B.C.E. is one of the oldest known human-made mummies.

Were Chinchorro mummies buried in tombs?

No. They were buried in shallow graves, sometimes with a few belongings such as a fishing line or a carved wooden statue. The faces of some Chinchorro mummies have been painted over many times, so scientists think these mummies were kept around for quite a while before they were buried. They might have been put on display or kept in the family home so relatives could mourn and pay their respects.

Both the Chinchorro and the Egyptians spent a lot of time and care on their mummies. Both cultures lived in places where they could get plenty of food, which left them time to develop their religions and to create elaborate mummies. Both believed that preserving the body meant the soul would survive, too. But unlike the Egyptians, the Chinchorro mummified everyone, not just the rich and powerful, with the same great care.

Yeah, go with the black. It's so classic!

Where have archaeologists found mummies all bundled up?

In an area of Peru called Paracas, which is just north of where the Chinchorro lived. The people of Paracas made mummies much later, and much differently, than the Chinchorro.

The Paracas people used cord to bind their dead in a seated position, with the body's legs tucked up against its chest. Then the body was covered with cloth or animal skin and wrapped in beautiful decorated fabric. The more important the person, the more layers of fabric he or she had. The cloth was woven by hand and often had pictures of birds, fish, or imaginary animals on it.

The Paracas people then placed the finished bundles on flat woven baskets and lowered them into large group burial chambers. More than four hundred human "mummy bundles," plus bundles containing cats, dogs, frogs, deer, parrots, and foxes, have been found in Paracas.

Mummy bundles made by the Chimu people of northern Peru about a thousand years ago had false heads that looked like square pillows. The head was made of stuffed cotton; and the eyes, nose, and mouth were fashioned of pieces of wood, copper, shell, or feathers.

If you were the mummy of an Inca king, where would you hang out?

a) on your throne
b) at a palace
c) at festivals and parades
d) all of the above

SOUTH AMERICA—
INCA MUMMIES

Boy, I needed an airing—and what the heck—I LOVE a parade!

The answer is *d*. The Inca empire flourished in what are now Peru, Bolivia, Ecuador, and Chile from about 1438 to 1532. The Inca mummified their dead leaders so they could continue to show them respect.

For at least a year after a ruler's death, his people treated him as if he were still alive. He stayed in his own palace, where servants brought him food and drink and sometimes new clothes. He was taken to important religious events and to visit other

The Spanish, who conquered the Inca empire in 1532, were troubled that the Inca worshipped their ancestors. The Spaniards were Christians, who worshipped only one god, and no spirits or ancestors. The leader of the Spanish conquerors, Francisco Pizarro, eventually ordered all royal Inca mummies burned.

royal mummies. At midsummer former Inca kings were dressed in beautiful clothes and masks and were paraded around on their thrones at the festival of Inti, the sun god. Since kings were thought to be descendants of Inti, in death the kings were supposed to act as messengers between the god and the Inca people. They made sure that Inti would allow summer to return every year.

How were Inca kings mummified?

No one knows exactly. They may have been taken high into the mountains, where the cold dry air would dry out their bodies. When a king had been dead a month, his mummy was placed in a burial vault. His old clothes and the hair and nail clippings from his lifetime were also put in the vault so that his spirit would not have to look for these things in death. His subjects then took the mummy out of the vault to the palace to be attended by servants.

Great! Nail clippings go just there. Now all we need is his hair!

The guy with the hair is right behind me!

In 1995 scientists found the mummy of a beautiful thirteen-year-old girl high in the Andes. They named her Juanita (and some reports called her the Ice Maiden). The scientists discovered her because hot ash from a volcano had melted five hundred years' worth of ice that had covered her body. They got Juanita down from the mountain as quickly as possible so that her mummy would not thaw out. In 1999 scientists found three more children, two girls and a boy, whose bodies were even better preserved. The younger girl's mummy had been struck by lightning. This loosened the fabric she was wrapped in and made it possible for scientists to see her face on the rocky mountaintop.

What did the Inca believe brought them good harvests?

The Inca believed that *sacrificing*, or giving up, precious things to Inti, the sun god, would bring rain and good harvests. So it was not only Inca kings who became mummies. In times of great danger, it was the Incas' most cherished gift of all—their children. It was a great honor to be chosen for sacrifice, which was performed high atop the Andes Mountains, closer to the sun god. At the top of the mountain, the child was wrapped in cloth and buried with extra clothing for the afterlife. Offerings of food and small statues were also included in the grave.

CHINESE MUMMIES

One of the most famous of the Tarim Basin mummies is Cherchen Man, named for the region in which he was found. Cherchen Man's clothes were as well preserved as his body. In fact, the salty desert sand made some of the dyes in his clothes brighter. Since colors usually fade with time, scientists were amazed by the dazzling reds, yellows, and blues of his striped leggings.

Where in China will you find a mummy mystery?

In the Taklimakan Desert in China's Tarim Basin, where more than one hundred mummies have been discovered. The bodies, buried between 2000 and 300 B.C.E., were naturally mummified because they were in bottomless coffins resting on desert salt beds. So what's so strange? The mummies look European, not Chinese. Most have fair hair, round eyes, long noses, and thick beards (on the men!), and wore European-style clothing. This puzzles scientists, who had thought that Europeans did not travel to China until about 110 B.C.E.

What ancient Chinese secret kept a noblewoman looking young?

Clay and charcoal, which kept tombs and coffins dry. In 1972 archaeologists found the burial chamber of a Chinese noblewoman sometimes called Lady Dai, who died around 168 B.C.E. Lady Dai's burial chamber, in a deep tomb in southeast China, was lined with layers of clay and charcoal. Inside the chamber charcoal lined a large wooden coffin as well. Inside the large coffin were five more beautifully painted coffins. In the innermost coffin was Lady Dai, wrapped in more than twenty layers of silk cloth. The noblewoman, whose body had been mummified in a bath of mercury salts, still had soft skin and a peaceful look on her face. Scientists who examined Lady Dai's body also discovered 138 whole watermelon seeds in her stomach!

Which Chinese royals were perfectly suited for death?

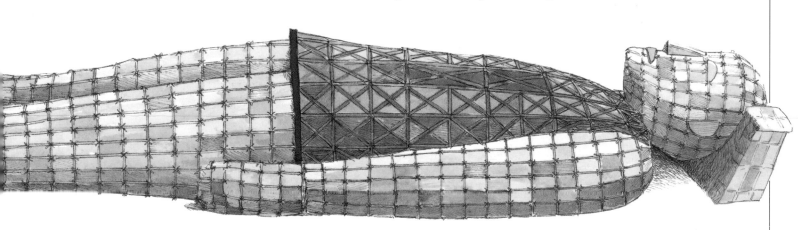

Prince Liu Sheng and his wife, Dou Wan, who ruled the area around what is now Beijing, China, from 145 to 113 B.C.E. The prince and princess were buried in huge tombs filled with jewels, silk, and carvings made of *jade*, a precious green stone. The tomb also held ten chariots and the skeletons of thirty horses. But archaeologists hoping to find the royals' bodies were disappointed. All they found were thousands of small pieces of jade lying on a table.

How do you know a mummy has a cold?

She starts coffin.

Liu Sheng and Dou Wan had been buried in beautiful jade suits. Each was made of more than two thousand small pieces of jade tied together with fine gold wire. The ancient Chinese believed that jade had magical powers that would protect and keep their bodies fresh forever. Even though the suits were so expertly made that they would have covered the bodies almost like soft cloth, they didn't preserve the bodies. (Charcoal would have been a better choice!) All that remained of the royal couple were a few of Liu Sheng's teeth.

How can you tell when a mummy is angry?

She flips her lid.

BOG MUMMIES

What can happen when people get really bogged down?

They can become mummies. A *bog* is an area of wet, spongy ground that's often covered with mud or patches of grass. It's easy to get "bogged down," or to sink into bogs the way you might sink into quicksand. Nearly fifteen hundred mummies have been found in the peat bogs of Great Britain, the Netherlands, Germany, and Scandinavia.

Bogs that are full of *peat*, or partly rotted plants and grass, preserve bodies especially well. That's because when peat rots, it releases special acids into the bog. The acids are like the ones used in tanning leather. So in a way, a person mummified in a peat bog turns into leather! (The mummies found in bogs do have a dark, leathery appearance.)

One reason so many mummies have been found in peat bogs is that people dig in them for fuel. Peat can be cut, dried, and burned in stoves.

How did bog mummies die?

Some died accidentally after sinking into the bog and drowning. Others died not so accidentally: They were hanged or stabbed. Were these people criminals who were executed? Were they offered as sacrifices?

One such mummy is Tollund Man, who was found in Denmark in 1950 by two men digging peat. Because the head they saw in the bog was so well preserved, the men thought it was that of a recent murder victim. But it turned out that Tollund Man was about two thousand years old. How did he die? He had a braided rope around his neck, so many people think this means he was hanged. Others say the rope was a religious symbol.

A mummy called Lindow Man, on the other hand, seems definitely to have been murdered by being strangled and hit on the head. Some people believe he may have been killed as a religious sacrifice.

What can we learn from a mummy's tummy?

More than you might think. By examining what's in a mummy's stomach, scientists can learn about more than the mummy's last meal. Lindow Man's stomach contained burnt bread. During the ancient spring festival of Beltane, people handed out pieces of a special bread. Whoever got the burnt portion was sacrificed to ensure a good harvest. Many other bog peoples' stomachs contain seeds and grains, which tell us that the people probably died in winter or early spring, when there were no fresh fruits or vegetables.

Is the Iceman a comic-book character?

No. (Not yet anyway.) The Iceman is a mummy found in 1991 in the mountains between Austria and Italy. He's 5,300 years old—which makes him one of the oldest fully preserved humans ever found.

The Iceman was well equipped and well dressed for the cold. He carried a copper ax, a bow and fourteen arrows, and a tool kit that included a dagger, a needle made of bone, and a piece of grass rope. He wore a fur hat and an animal-skin coat and leggings. He also wore a windproof grass cape and deerskin shoes filled with grass to prevent frostbite. The Iceman's clothes and belongings tell scientists a lot about life in Europe in his day.

ICE MUMMIES

No one really knows what the Iceman was doing so high in the mountains, but scientists do know how he died. In 2001 they used a *CT scan*, a kind of three-dimensional X ray, and found a flint arrowhead buried in his left shoulder. (See more about CT scans on page 44.) Apparently the Iceman was shot from behind—whether in a war, or in a personal fight, no one knows—and eventually died on the cold, dry mountainside.

huh ?

Where was the mummy of an infant mistaken for a doll?

In Greenland. Hans Grønvold found eight Inuit mummies—including that of a six-month-old baby—while hunting with his brother in 1972. (The Inuit are the native peoples of Greenland and northern Canada.) Grønvold wrote, "We saw a doll which had fallen to the side, a doll which turned out to be a little child."

The eight mummies were well preserved at the foot of a cliff, where they had been protected from wind and rain and mummified by the cold, dry air. The Inuit, who probably died around 1475, were well prepared for the afterlife in warm clothes made of animal skin. (They believed that a person's soul needed warm clothes for the long journey to the land of the dead.) Many of the women had tattoos on their faces, as was the custom for married women. No one knows how the eight people died, or if they died at the same time. But their clothing and bodies have told scientists about Greenland's past.

Are all mummies from long ago?

No. British mountain climbers George Mallory and Andrew Irvine, who were trying to reach the top of Mount Everest in 1924, are among the many modern climbers who have frozen to death on mountains. Mallory's well-preserved body was found in 1999, but in keeping with the custom of Everest climbers, it was left where it lay. Climbers are still looking for Irvine's body.

The body of a sailor named John Torrington, mummified in his coffin, was examined in 1984. Torrington was a member of a British expedition through the Canadian Arctic. He and all the other members of his crew probably died in the winter of 1845–1846 after being weakened by lead poisoning from the cans their food was stored in.

OTHER MUMMIES

Is a *catacomb* a hairbrush for your favorite pet?

No, a catacomb is an underground cemetery that preserves bodies in its cold, dry air. One of the most famous catacombs is in Palermo, on the Italian island of Sicily. Starting more than four hundred years ago, Sicilians began preserving the bodies of local people by drying them in front of a slow-burning fire, then storing them in a catacomb. Relatives saw the mummies as a direct link to their ancestors. Parents packed picnic lunches and brought children to pray, talk, and visit with their dead relatives.

Eight thousand mummies survive in Palermo today. No one has been mummified for more than eighty years, but people can still tour the catacomb. The monks who give the tours also look after the mummies, giving the bodies a gentle cleaning with a vacuum cleaner once a year. (How would you like that chore?)

Where have mummies been found in North America?

In caves. In the American Southwest, ancestors of today's Native Americans were buried in caves as much as nineteen hundred years ago. Some became natural mummies in the caves' dry soil, high temperatures, and low humidity.

People have also found many human-made mummies in the warm, dry caves of the Aleutian Islands of Alaska. The Aleuts removed a dead person's internal organs, stuffed the body with grass, and tied it in a crouched position. They may also have dried the bodies in smoke to speed the mummification process.

Did mummies ever hang out in tree houses?

Yes. In Indonesia people placed dead bodies in trees to be dried by the sun. Sometimes they tied them to a bamboo stretcher and placed them above a fire to be smoke-dried. The mummies were laid to rest in caves and other openings in the earth, which many people believed were entrances to the next world.

Drink up!

Some tribes in Australia used a similar mummification process. But instead of putting their finished mummies in caves, Australians kept them with their families for a generation or two. They gave the skull to the nearest relative to be used as a drinking cup.

Which people horsed around with their mummies?

The Scythians, who were warlike wanderers living near the Black Sea, in present-day Russia, between 700 and 300 B.C.E. The Scythians spent almost all their time on horseback and were excellent riders. They mummified important people by removing their internal organs and stuffing the bodies with *frankincense* (a sweet-smelling resin), parsley, and hair. Then they buried their mummies in deep, wood-lined tombs covered with tall earth mounds. A year after the burial, fifty of the dead person's attendants and fifty horses were killed, mummified, and laid to rest in horse-and-rider pairs in a large circular grave around the burial mound.

The Guanche people of the Canary Islands, off the northwest coast of Africa, mummified their upper-class citizens. They placed them in caves, either lying down flat, standing straight up, hanging from the walls, or sewn up in goatskins. Between 1402 and 1773 thousands of Guanche mummies were found in caves. Few remain today because most were ground up to make mummy powder (see page 23).

LEARNING FROM MUMMIES

Why do scientists and historians study mummies?

Because even though mummies can't talk out loud, they have a lot to tell us. For a long time people didn't think of studying mummies. They looted their graves or unwrapped them and threw the mummies and their wrappings away. But today scientists try to preserve mummies and take good care of them. We know that mummies, as well as the places they're buried and the things they're buried with, can reveal a great deal about a people's rituals, beliefs, art, technology, and way of life.

Ooh! Nice amulet!

Do we have to unwrap mummies to examine them?

No, not anymore. Scientists used to unwrap mummies and cut them open to learn what was inside. But the invention of X-ray analysis in 1895 changed that. X rays allow scientists to peek inside a mummy without harming the body. An X ray gives scientists a flat picture that shows bones and other hard objects. Today, an advanced X-ray process called CT scanning can show us a "virtual mummy." CT scans take hundreds of separate picture "slices" that are combined by a computer to form a 3-D image. CT scans show all the mummy's surfaces, inside and out.

This doesn't mean scientists don't ever unwrap and take tiny samples from a mummy's bandages and body. Sometimes they want to examine a mummy's skin, organs, and muscle cells. They can take skin samples from the underside of a mummy, where the marks will be hidden from sight. Organ samples from Egyptian mummies are often taken through the original embalmer's slit or from organs that have been preserved separately from the mummy.

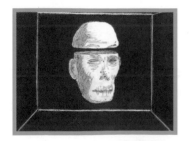

What can scientists learn from mummies' bodies?

For starters, bones and teeth can tell us a lot. They can show how old a mummified person was when he or she died, especially if death occurred before age twenty-five, when bones and teeth are still growing. Bones and teeth can also reveal information about a mummified person's health and diet. Egyptian mummies have been found with broken bones and arthritis. Most had teeth that were worn down because of the grainy bread the person ate and the sand that blew into their food. Some mummies' teeth were so worn down or decayed that the person suffered an infection that probably killed them.

A mummy's blood and tissue samples can tell us even more about that person's diseases. Looking at Egyptian mummy tissue under microscopes, scientists have found cancer cells and a lung disease caused by breathing in too much desert sand. Sometimes cells are in good enough condition that scientists can make out the mummy's *DNA*, or the "code" that exists in nearly every one of a body's cells. DNA is like a recipe for what the cell does and how it works. It can reveal certain diseases as well as who was related to whom.

How did researchers work backward to learn about Egyptian mummies?

Instead of taking an ancient mummy apart, two researchers *made* a mummy. At the University of Maryland in 1994, the researchers used the body of a recently deceased man and applied what they knew of the Egyptian mummifying process. They even got natron and oils from Egypt. It worked! When the mummy was finished, the leader of the project said that the hardest part of making a mummy was getting the brain out through the nose.

A scientist who studied lung tissue from a mummy in Peru found evidence of a disease called *tuberculosis*. Tuberculosis is very contagious, and people in Asia, Africa, and Europe suffered from it for thousands of years. Scientists once thought it was Europeans who brought the disease to North and South America. The mummy showed that the disease was already there when Europeans arrived. Learning how ancient diseases spread can help scientists understand how modern diseases are passed on.

MUMMIES TODAY

Could you become a mummy?

Yes. You can pay a company in Salt Lake City, Utah, to embalm and wrap you, Egyptian style, when you die. You can even mummify your pet. The company will seal you in a mummy-shaped coffin, with or without hieroglyphics telling the story of your life. No one has been mummified by the company yet, but several people who are still living have signed up.

Gold leaf glyphs are extra, of course...

Another modern mummification technique is *cryogenic suspension*, which keeps bodies preserved in tanks of super-cooled liquid gas. A few very rich people have had their bodies chilled this way, hoping that when scientists find a cure for the disease that killed them, they might be restored to life—if scientists figure out how to do *that*, too.

You can also donate your body to science and hope you might be mummified for use in medical schools. A process called *plastination* preserves a body's soft tissues by replacing the water in them with plastic. This gives medical students a first-hand look inside the human body.

The 1920s and 1930s saw the beginning of mummy movie madness. The world was learning about King Tut, and horror movies were becoming popular. For instance, in the 1932 film *The Mummy*, archaeologists accidentally wake up an Egyptian mummy, who then wanders about, trailing bandages, while he searches for his long-lost love. Mummies coming back to life have been a favorite topic of writers and movie-makers, but—sorry, folks—it can't happen in real life.

Where can you go (besides the movies) to see mummies?

It's easy to forget that mummies were once real people. Mummies were never meant to be unwrapped and viewed by the world, but the museums that display them today do so with the utmost respect.

The best Egyptian mummies are in the Egyptian Museum in Cairo. If you can't get there, other museums also have Egyptian and non-Egyptian mummies. Try:

The **Field Museum of Natural History** in Chicago, IL. It has a permanent exhibit called "Inside Ancient Egypt" that includes twenty-three human mummies and a reconstruction of an Egyptian tomb.

The **San Diego Museum of Man** in San Diego, CA. It has mummies from Mexico as well as Peru and other South American countries.

The **Brooklyn Museum of Art** in Brooklyn, NY. This museum has an excellent collection of Egyptian art. It includes sarcophagi, coffins, mummy cases, and a wrapped mummy.

The **Metropolitan Museum of Art** in New York City, which has many mummy cases, three mummies, and a large collection of Egyptian art.

The **Denver Museum of Nature & Science** in Denver, CO. It has an exhibit that takes you step-by-step through the mummification process and displays coffins, grave goods, and both human and animal mummies.

The **Museum of Fine Arts** in Boston, MA. This museum has a mummy and her three wooden coffins as well as grave goods from several burial sites.

The **University of Memphis Institute of Egyptian Art and Archaeology** in Memphis, TN. Here you'll find the coffin, death mask, and mummy of a man named Iret-irew (EAR-et EAR-oo).

The **University of Pennsylvania Museum** in Philadelphia, PA, where you'll see objects and materials used in the mummification process, grave goods, and both human and animal mummies, including that of a pet dog.

The **Rosicrucian Egyptian Museum** in San Jose, CA. This has an extensive collection of human and animal mummies, canopic jars, *ushabtis*, a funerary boat, and the replica of a tomb. The museum itself is modeled after an Egyptian temple.

TIME LINE OF NATURAL AND HUMAN-MADE MUMMIES

A c. before a date means "circa," or "about."

c. 310 million years ago	An insect is preserved in amber; it will become the oldest mummy ever found
c. 34,000 B.C.E.	Blue Babe dies in present-day Alaska
c. 5000–1500 B.C.E.	Chinchorro mummies made in Chile
c. 3300 B.C.E.	Iceman dies in the Alps
c. 3100 B.C.E.–c. 400 C.E.	Mummies made in Egypt
c. 2566 B.C.E.	Great Pyramid completed at Giza, Egypt
c. 1327 B.C.E.	Tutankhamen buried in the Valley of the Kings
c. 1213 B.C.E.	Ramses II buried in the Valley of the Kings
c. 700–300 B.C.E.	Scythians bury their chiefs and noblemen in present-day Russia
c. 400–200 B.C.E.	Paracas mummies made in Peru
c. 400 B.C.E.–c. 400 C.E.	People die in peat bogs of Great Britain, the Netherlands, Germany, and Scandinavia
c. 1438–1532	Inca mummify their dead rulers in Peru
c. 1475	Inuit in Greenland mummified near a dry rocky cliff
c. 1600–1920	Sicilians mummify and place the dead in catacombs
1924	George Mallory and Andrew Irvine die on Mount Everest